I0480574

INSTAGRAM:

How To Build Your Business And Increase Sales

Instagram Marketing Tips to Enhance Your Business

Table of Contents

INSTAGRAM - A BOOMING PLATFORM FOR A SOCIAL MEDIA MARKETING PLATFORM

One of the best things that social media has brought to digital marketing is that it has allowed businesses to communicate with their target market in a platform where they are always present. Moreover, it has given them a way to obtain powerful insights from the accurate data that can gathered from activities on social media.

Instagram is one of these platforms. It has become one of the most popular photo-sharing apps and this is why many businesses have already considered using the platform to help increase awareness about a specific campaign or to enhance their business overall. Let's take a look at the ways in which Instagram can help your business:

1. Use unique, crisp, and attractive hashtags

Hashtags are not only important for Twitter; they also play a prominent role on Instagram. It helps potential customers find you through their Instagram searches. In comparison with Twitter, here you're not restricted by character count.

You can include a few hashtags in your posts to get connected. In deciding on hashtags for branding, it is advisable to create brand specific hashtags. Try to keep it as unique yet brand specific as possible. Try multiple variant of hashtags such as brand specific hashtags, general hashtags, and trending hashtags, to get noticed in searches.

Examples of brand specific hashtags are:

- #PutACanOnIt - Red Bull
- #TweetFromTheSeat - Charmin
- #OreoHorrorStories - Oreos
- #WantAnR8 - Audi

An ideal general hashtag should be prepared with two words over a single word to make it meaningful e.g. #AskQL is a better than using #QL as a hashtag.

2. Consistently interact with your followers

Once you begin to get followers, do not shy away from being engaged. Try to constantly post impressive content which your followers find relevant to their interest and can associate with your business. Avoid throwing up random posts on your feed.

At least, twice a day posting is requisite. Once your followers start increasing, you can start posting three to four times a day.

Consistency matters most! According to Anthony Carbone, "If you stick to a niche and show authenticity and passion in your posts, you will find a strong following"

The more people you can dynamically involve and persuade to comment on your content (images/videos), the better for you. Since, it will inculcate the interest for others who want to contribute or comment on your content as well.

3. Do not bore your audience with information overload

Consistency is important, but if it lacks harmony and relevancy, it results in either spamming or information overload. Keep your frequency correct and consistent. Rather than preaching, so to speak, engage with your audience. Your audience should feel valued. Seek meaningful interaction from them.

4. Make the most use of tools that are free

Instagram also provides free analytics tools for business profiles; make the most use of these tools to market your products and services. For example, "insights", an analytical tool, provides access to engagement data. If your account is a personal account for your business, switch to a business profile. That's how you can take advantage of the free tools that businesses use to shape their brand on Instagram. 'Insights' helps you understand your audience, provides you data on posts with most impressions, engagements, and shares. Ultimately, you will conclude which posts are effective and which ones are not working well with your audience.

5. Repurpose content from other related sources

As stated in earlier, effective and successful Instagram marketing requires consistent posts related to your products and services. It can be difficult to come up with creative and engaging posts, it's not EASY! That's where re-purposing content or curating content offers a hand. Providing you either tag or mention the original poster, this is a completely ethical marketing practice and does not fall under the cloud of plagiarism. However, to reiterate you must make sure to ensure that the posts which you choose to repurpose or curate are relevant to your followers.

Social media marketing via Instagram can facilitate you to achieve your targeted business goals.

Basically:

Use Instagram to grow bigger!!!

IS INSTAGRAM GOOD FOR MARKETING YOUR BUSINESS?

To date, there are more than 300 million users on Instagram - most of which are more affluent and younger than users on any other social media platform. Not to mention, people are using their mobile devices more to engage with brands and to purchase a company's products online.

Many small businesses are turning to social media and mobile advertising to help create curiosity, grow their brand and ultimately SELL MORE PRODUCTS! Instagram is great for both physical and online products and services. It's become a place where users are ready, willing and able to purchase right on the spot with their mobile devices.

Instagram has also become a measurable driver of both lead generation and sales and has become one of the most popular social media ad platforms helping small businesses reach millions of targeted customers and cash in on its supercharged targeting capabilities.

It is also a great place to gain an exclusive following where you can share information about new products, new features or new services. And now with the integration of Instagram Ads you can expand your reach with very little effort and a small budget.

Whether you're running ads or not, if you're promoting your product in a niche market that isn't really profitable, you're probably wasting your time and money. Sinking money into advertising that doesn't produce a positive ROI (return on investment) is not only frustrating but also very common for small businesses. Unfortunately, the problem may not be the way you are marketing your product, but to whom you are marketing to.

Not all niche markets are created equally. The truth is some niche markets are just more profitable than others. The goal is to be in a niche that is making money. If you are spending time and money marketing within a large, saturated market, it's likely you'll stand out! Be more specific with the targeting of your product and message.

There's no denying that promoting your offer in a niche market with lots of buyers spending money is a good business decision. For business owners the bottom line is what matters and there are several benefits of marketing in a profitable niche market. One is, you'll make money!

Another, you'll be able to provide valuable products the market will **tell you** it wants.

Using Instagram to market a product in the wrong niche market is one of the biggest mistakes small businesses make, so take time to dig deeper into your niche market and research to deliver what people want – now that's good marketing.

REASONS WHY YOU SHOULD BE USING INSTAGRAM FOR YOUR BUSINESS?

Instagram is a social networking app that was designed to let you share videos and photos online. Most people think that it's just a way for people to share their holiday snaps or what they're eating with friends.

But Instagram has become a social media powerhouse. It's become a great place for businesses and brands to connect with their followers and increase sales. In one month over 120 million people on Instagram will visit a website, get directions, call, email, or send a direct message to learn about a business based on what they saw on Instagram.

Easy to Use

Instagram is incredibly easy for anyone to use. Even if you don't have a lot of experience when it comes to social media websites, you'll find that Instagram has a very user-friendly interface that you will learn to use effectively in no time. It's a great way to give your business a bit of personality and spark some customer interest.

It's Free

You generally have to spend money when it comes to tools and resources to improve and grow your business, but you can set up Instagram account for free by downloading the app onto your smartphone or tablet. There are no limitations. You also don't need to spend any money to create a business profile.

Valuable Insights

A business profile on Instagram enables you to obtain valuable insight into your followers. This is unique information only available to owners of business accounts. You'll find out more information about who your followers are and when they're online.

Reach a Huge Audience

It cannot be stressed enough, MILLIONS of people (potential customers) around the globe use Instagram every day. Using hashtags makes it easy to get your posts in front of people looking for particular things pertaining to your business, products or services, but who may not be following you yet.

Get Creative!

Getting a business profile on Instagram will make it possible for you to get creative with the videos and photos that you publish. You must post unique, quality content if you want your business to be a hit on Instagram.

You can get creative by using Instagram stories. It's a feature that allows you to post a photo or video but it's only available for 24 hours. After that, it's gone. Because they are not around forever, people are encouraged to view and share them quickly. For businesses, Instagram stories have great potential and can be used to boost business if used strategically. This is where your insights come in handy. Your insights will be able to give you some indication on the best time to post in your stories.

Research shows that consumers are 58 times more likely to engage with branded content on Instagram compared to Facebook, and 120 times more likely to take some action than users on Twitter.

INSTAGRAM MARKETING TIPS FOR YOUR BUSINESS

Tell the Story Using Photos and Videos

Photos are worth a thousand words and Instagram is all about pictures. If you are on Instagram for marketing purposes, then you ought to understand that random photos aren't effective. Posting pictures of your products is one of the best ways of increasing your brand awareness and boost sales of your products. The pictures do not necessarily need to be very professional. The key thing is having the pictures highlight the main features and functions of the goods you are promoting.

Videos are also important in Instagram marketing. You can create and share a video with your employees to promote the product at hand. You can also opt to do a live product review video and share it on Instagram. Pictures and videos are more appealing to many people than text. Media files stand higher chances of going viral as people share them. They are also more memorable. Create photos and videos that show your brand story and values. Images and videos are important if you want to improve your brand and sales.

Use Quality Media

To improve your visibility, try to share high-quality photos and videos in your feeds. You can of course seek professional assistance or advice from a photographer. However, you can also use a great camera such as your iPhone to take sharp pictures. Try to get your images at best angles. Edit your photos for better results. Nowadays mobile phones are equipped with photo editing tools for this purpose. Instagram too has several photo editing tools. Utilize these tools for your Instagram marketing purpose.

Connect with your Followers

Maintaining contact with your customers is vital, particularly for developing a business with a small market share. You can start by showing your clients that you are concerned about their feedback. You can achieve this by replying to their questions and comments. This will improve user-generated content and credibility as well as promote the visibility of your products and business. Your Instagram followers can significantly influence the success of your enterprise – don't underestimate them!

Use Branded Hashtags

You should include your business name in you hashtags. Use unique hashtags for a particular promotional campaign. Not only does this promote your campaign, but it also provides a unique hashtag for your clients to connect and share with other participants.

Adopt a Friendly Attitude Towards Everyone

While carrying out your Instagram marketing, you need to understand that Instagram is a community composed of people with varied ideas, emotions, and backgrounds. Always be friendly to everyone and appreciate the time they took to connect with you on your page. Always ensure you listen to your customers.

Be Active

Post at least once daily to keep things up to date and ensure your followers updated with the current happenings. You can experiment posting at varying times of the day to see which time your posts do best.

Consistency

Consistency is crucial in Instagram marketing. Be consistent in your postings and develop a theme that is prominent in your posts. Let your followers know what to expect from you.

Link your Instagram and Facebook Accounts

Connect your Instagram and Facebook accounts to improve your marketing power. Nowadays, you can have an Instagram tab on your Facebook page. This allows you to share your Instagram posts to your Facebook followers if you have a fan page.

You can network with friends and the world via Instagram. Instagram can be used for marketing purposes. Instagram marketing can improve your brand's visibility, increase sales, and consequently your revenue.

INSTAGRAM MARKETING: BUILDING BRAND AWARENESS AND FOLLOWERS

With the integration and growing importance of social signals to the Google algorithm, you are encouraged to use social media platforms to skyrocket your advertising efforts. One of the tools that have been gaining considerable attention from SEO specialists and internet marketers is Instagram. But like any other business strategy, you can't just jump onto the bandwagon and see results. The formula is to build brand awareness and gain more followers.

Instagram has taken the lead in making the web more visual, creating avid photographers from average users and brand specialists from businesses who have seen the potential of such platform. Photo-sharing has proven to be a great way to attract a good following, increase customer relations, and inspire active participation and discussion from users. To enjoy all these promising benefits, what does it take to make your marketing campaign a success?

1. Set up and manage your account professionally

If you are not outsourcing social media optimization, you have to take the time to set up and manage an account... professionally. Think of how you would want people to remember and see your business. One good Instagram marketing strategy to look into is that of Burberry's - a British luxury fashion brand. Among the photos that they share are taken during their events, behind the scenes. By doing so, they allow their followers to enjoy the "experience" through insider photos of glitz and glamour. This involvement ignites interest and sharing.

2. Set up schedules

No internet user would want to follow an account that uploads 30 photos at a time, each day. Though flooding your feed with everything you have in your photo album can be a tempting thought, this move can also lead to annoying your followers who may decide to unfollow your account and even marking your posts as spam. Instead, focus on quality and creativity, and your one single photo would be able to bring your message across more efficiently than the longest article you can write.

3. Upload Actual Photos

The success of your Instagram marketing campaign lies heavily on the creativity of your photos. Share real, creative photos and if you have to include some text then that is what the captions are for. And if you are having a hard time figuring out what to post next, here are several ideas for content strategy:

- **Images of your products in various sets or backdrops.**

- **Images of people, famous or average, using your products- can be the usual, candid, funny, or unconventional.**

HOW TO CREATE INSTAGRAM POSTS THAT INCREASE SALES

Keep in mind, that using Instagram for marketing should be more than just taking photos, applying filters and publishing them on your news feed. You can still take several steps to ensure your photos stand out and you attract more attention.

Design Your Photos

When you're sharing images of your products, it is best to be more creative when taking shots of them. Look for different angles from the usual or you can include another item together with your product. You may also add text to your photo to grab more attention.

Proper lighting is a must. Whether you're snapping photos indoors or outdoors, do keep lighting in mind. Lighting is crucial in telling a story about your product so make sure to use light properly.

Decide also whether you want to share certain photos in color or simply in black and white. And consider using Instagram's filters as well.

Include a Caption

While a photo already speaks a thousand words, adding a well-written caption can attract more attention from Instagram users. Think of a caption that best describes the image and the story you would like to convey.

Include a Call to Action

Including a call to action to your post helps encourage your followers and potential customers to take action. This step is also effective in gaining new followers.

Remember to create a call to action that easily grabs attention and can prompt people to act immediately while viewing your image.

Take note of these tips every time you post an image on Instagram and you can be sure to attract more potential customers and improve your sales moving forward.

3 STEPS FOR EFFECTIVE INSTAGRAM MARKETING

Instagram is increasing in popularity among brands as a powerful social marketing tool. People today enjoy being visually stimulated, which makes a social network that is solely based on image sharing so effective.

When you use social media to share images that relate to your business, you will forge stronger relationships with your current followers and customers, plus broaden your reach to find new ones. Not only can you share pictures of your products and the people who work hard to keep your business running (even if it's just you and your pet ferret!), but you can encourage your customers to submit their own pictures of your products being put to use.

It is easy to lose track of time when you log in to your social media accounts. This is especially true with Instagram, where you can easily lose an hour just scanning through the wide variety of images in your stream. Spending time online is important for your business, but if it's not productive time, then it is simply time wasted. Wasted time does not help bring in new sales. This is why you need to have daily goals for each of your social network activity like when you log on to Instagram.

Before you start your day, know how much time you want to allot to social media and each individual network. Stick with that time limit so that you can be sure you are getting the most important tasks done in your time frame and don't allow yourself to get sucked in to the rabbit hole that is the Internet.

Each time you log on to Instagram, make sure you are doing these three things to maintain a high level of efficiency to grow your brand presence:

Add to the Number of People You Follow

Give yourself about 10-15 minutes each day to start looking for Instagram users in your target market. You can do this by looking at who is following your competitors. Find people who are more engaging with the brands they follow since they are more likely to engage with you as well. Are they leaving comments and liking photos often?

Since social media is all about give and take, make sure that you are following a good number of other people and businesses and bloggers. Do your own fair share of liking and commenting as well.

Share Your Own Content

Take 10 minutes a day to add new unique content to your own Instagram account. People want to see that you have a good amount of interesting content for them to look at if they are going to follow you. If they look at your stream and only see two pictures and nothing new added in the last month or more, they aren't going to see a reason to become a follower.

If you don't have any unique content to share, set up a time each day to simply focus on taking pictures to share. It can be shots of your products, your office, employees, etc. If it relates to your brand and business, take an interesting shot of it and edit it to your liking and share.

Be Interactive

It's no surprise that when you have a social media account, people expect you to be, well, social. Don't simply sign up for an account and then wait for people to start following you.

To be successful in your Instagram marketing, you need to be actively engaging. Reply to comments left on your images, even if it's a simple thank you. Ask questions and encourage a dialog with your followers.

Visit your followers' streams and those of the people that you are following and like images and leave comments. Showing that you will be interactive with other users will go a long way in building your own brand's following.

Instagram will be around for a long time. To be the most effective, you need to be ready to spend time on your account and be productive with that time.

3 WAYS YOU CAN USE INSTAGRAM TO BOOST YOUR BRAND'S IMAGE

The single most common problem facing businesses is driving traffic to their website and in turn getting more conversions or sales. While you might get hits on your website, there is no guarantee they will turn into sales or conversions for your business. You need to create a solid brand image before and build credibility with respect to your brand and business before you can see conversions in large numbers.

It is a given fact that visuals attract more attention than text. So, there's no reason why businesses who would do well with an Instagram profile wouldn't want to capitalize on this opportunity. Also, Instagram, in the literal sense of the word, makes your business 'look' good. Imagine the reactions of your audience when you upload pictures of your products, team members, and general engagement images. They'll be excited to be able to see all of this.

There are many other ways you can use Instagram to promote your brand and business.

Here we list 4 ways you can use Instagram to boost your brand's image.

Use Tagged URLs

When you upload pictures related to your business or products, it is a good idea to insert links to your website in a manner that the URL can be tracked through analytics. This way, you know there is traffic being driven from Instagram to your website and probably resulting in conversions for your business.

Competitions and Contests

Instagram contests with giveaways unique to your business makes for a great brand audience engagement technique. More than the contest in itself, it will be the prizes that the winners receive that will attract your audience toward the contest and your Instagram account in general. Contests where you ask the participants to tag your Instagram account when uploading the entries is a sure way of getting people to notice your brand and get new followers in the process.

Give a Sneak Peek to your Followers

Your customers will be curious to know about the latest products being launched by your company. Apart from this, your audience will also want to a glimpse of the behind-the-scene working of your business. So, feed their curiosity with glimpses of your office which should also ideally include pictures of various teams working.

While Instagram is usually overlooked as a 'not-so-useful' social media platform, it has the potential to give your brand instant recognition, provided its features are explored and utilized to the maximum.

SIMPLE TIPS TO ENHANCE YOUR INSTAGRAM STRATEGY

Instagram is one of the leading social media platforms on the Web today, so it makes sense that a lot of small businesses are finding unique ways to use it to boost their own sales. At first glance, Instagram may not appear to be a great venue for marketing your products and/or services, but with an SEO expert on your squad, you can find a way to do so successfully. Social media is a place where you can not only advertise your brand, but build it up as well. Online reputation management and social media management are sometimes left up to professional services.

And if you already have an Instagram strategy in place, but it's not performing as you thought it would, and then the following tips can be used to give it a nudge in the right direction.

Go Beyond Audience and Isolate Behaviors

If you've done your research, you know that a majority of Instagram users are between 18 and 29 years old (53 percent to be exact). It's also been noted that there are more women than men using Instagram, showing a seven percent difference. Tidbits of data like this can help give perspective to the potential audiences you can reach, but what's really important to look at is the behavior of your audience.

How do they interact with your brand? Keep track of the messages you receive and monitor hashtag performance to see which keywords are generating the most participation.

Find out who is Unfollowing You

It's just as important to know who's unfollowing you as it is to know who's following you. If you notice certain demographics are clicking the "unfollow" button, then it's time to learn why. You can gather intel about unfollowers using tools like Crowdfire. You can also find an expert who offers SEO services to analyze the data and determine what should be done to prevent more unfollows.

Push Out Relevant Posts

Instagram isn't for every business, but you'll be surprised how many companies in various industries have been successful, including those in real estate, retail, food service and so on. If the posts you make aren't relevant to your audience, then they're not going to pay attention, let alone follow you. Make sure that you are offering an experience that your audience finds valuable. You can post photos, how-to videos and even user-generated content. If you need help with coming up with a strategy, you can hire an SEO expert that offers social media management services.

5 PHOTO TIPS TO BOOST YOUR INSTAGRAM MARKETING

Instagram has 52 times greater engagement level than Facebook and 127 times greater than Twitter. What this means is there's a substantial opportunity for businesses to market a wide range of products and services on Instagram to get maximum sales and profits.

Your Instagram page is a way to make a great first impression on any potential prospects. And the best way to make an awesome first impression is take great photos and videos.

1. Lighting

Bear in mind that no amount of filtering or editing will save a photo that's badly lit. Use natural light whenever you can, except in cases where you have access to the right kind of lighting set- up. If you're taking pictures outside, early morning and late afternoon are the best times.

2. Use Your Eyes

Before you take out your phone and start snapping pictures, take a moment to really look at what's going on around you. Use your eyes to structure the photo in your mind. Don't just take out your smart phone and start snapping.

What's in the background of the photo? Is someone about to walk in front of your subject? Is there something going on nearby that might mean taking this picture in a different location would be a better idea? Spend some time looking at your subject, your surroundings, lighting and everything else that is going on before you start clicking away.

3. Use Technology

Instagram provides a variety of filters and editing tools. There are also third-party apps which improve the capability of your smart phone camera. There's nothing improper with using apps and tools to take good pictures. Most smart phones have some kind of photo adjusting features and built into their cameras.

They usually include tools that let you cut, switch, modify lighting and contrast levels, increase or decrease saturation, add shadows, shades and highlights and create the long exposure effects.

4. Move around Your Subject

The lens of smart phone camera soaks up light in a different way in comparison to a traditional camera. When looking through your phone at your subject while moving through a full circle, you'll see how the shifting direction of your light sources can uncover some fantastic effects, and surprising results. You'll start to observe opportunities that previously didn't occur when you just held your phone up and clicked a picture.

5. Change Your Viewpoint

Shooting from up high or right down on the ground can result in more interesting pictures and makes your pictures to them look different. Photos that stand out get shared. This is how a single photograph on Instagram can go viral, earn you hundreds or even thousands of followers, and help you draw attention to your business.

COMMON MYTHS ABOUT USING INSTAGRAM FOR BUSINESS

Undoubtedly, Instagram is one of the biggest and most powerful social media platforms that help to boost traffic to your website. This platform helps you to generate new leads for your business. It earns an enormous popularity in a very short span and now become the first choice of every business person. It allows you to share pictures, videos and do much more things on it either publicly or privately.

Instagram is for customers and not for brands

You are mistaken. No platform is better than Instagram for driving more traffic to your website. It allows you to share the images and videos related to your products and services, which then helps to boost sales. Big brands like Blackberry, FedEx, National Geographic and many others are already using this platform for their business, so, you should dismiss this myth.

Instagram only works if you sell visual products

Another misconception is that it only works if you sell visual product. No matter if you sell a hairpin or a helicopter you can use this platform for the branding or generating more leads for your business.

It doesn't allow you to showcase your personality

Lie! - Instagram is very popular for behind the scenes looks, so, it definitely allows you to showcase your actual personality among your customers.

Results can't measure

Instagram doesn't enable you to monitor or track your activity. What? Another Myth! No, it's not true; it has a built-in analytical tool that helps you to keep an eye on your social media activity, so you don't need to worry about the monitoring.

Instagram has lots more to offer for your business if you use it in a right way, so, don't underestimate its power and start using it, TODAY!

www.ingramcontent.com/pod-product-compliance
Lightning Source LLC
Chambersburg PA
CBHW030546220526
45463CB00007B/2999